20 COLOR-CODED XYLOPH MELODIES
Color-Coded Beginner Xylophone Sheet Music

This book was written to help an absolute beginner, whether child or adult, learn to play the xylophone in a simple and easy way that requires no knowledge of reading music. Just by following the color circles, you will sound like an experienced musician. Playing music can be as simple and enjoyable as a game. That is our goal: to give you what's necessary to play beautiful music while having fun.

For good sound, it is necessary to learn to freely hold the mallets, and to strike the keys of the xylophone lightly, aiming for the center of each key. This percussion instrument develops not only the ears, but gross and fine motor skills and cognitive skills such as letter recognition, matching, and patterns.

All melodies in this book were simplified for a 1-octave diatonic xylophone.

The color of the keys on your 8 note xylophone must be the same as the color of the xylophone keys on the cover.

For some melodies, we group circles to show rhythm.

Recommended for ages 3 and up.

The small blue circle corresponds to the small blue key on the xylophone, and the big circle to the big key.

The arrangement of the bars is from low (longer bars) to high (shorter bars).

Contents

1. Hot Cross Buns
2. Are You Sleeping?
3. Mary Had a Little Lamb
4. The Wheels on the Bus
5. Twinkle, Twinkle, Little Star
6. Old MacDonald Had a Farm
7. Do You Know the Muffin Man?
8. London Bridge is Falling Down
9. Jingle Bells
10. We Wish You a Merry Christmas
11. Brahms' Lullaby (Lullaby and Goodnight)
12. Ode to Joy
13. Happy Birthday
14. La Cucaracha
15. Oh! Susannah
16. Itsy Bitsy Spider
17. The First Noel
18. Yankee Doodle
19. Row, Row, Row Your Boat
20. Jolly Old Saint Nicholas
21. Amazing Grace (Bonus)

Hot Cross Buns

E D C
Hot Cross Buns,

E D C
Hot Cross Buns,

C C C C
One a pen - ny,

D D D D
Two a pen - ny,

E D C
Hot Cross Buns.

Hot Cross Buns,
Hot Cross Buns,
One a penny,
Two a penny,
Hot Cross Buns.

1

Are You Sleeping?

C D E C C D E C
Are you sleeping, are you sleeping?

E F G E F G
Brother John, Brother John?

G A G F E C
Morning bells are ringing,

G A G F E C
Morning bells are ringing

D G C D G C
Ding ding dong, ding ding dong.

Are you sleeping, are you sleeping?
Brother John, Brother John?
Morning bells are ringing,
Morning bells are ringing
Ding ding dong, ding ding dong.

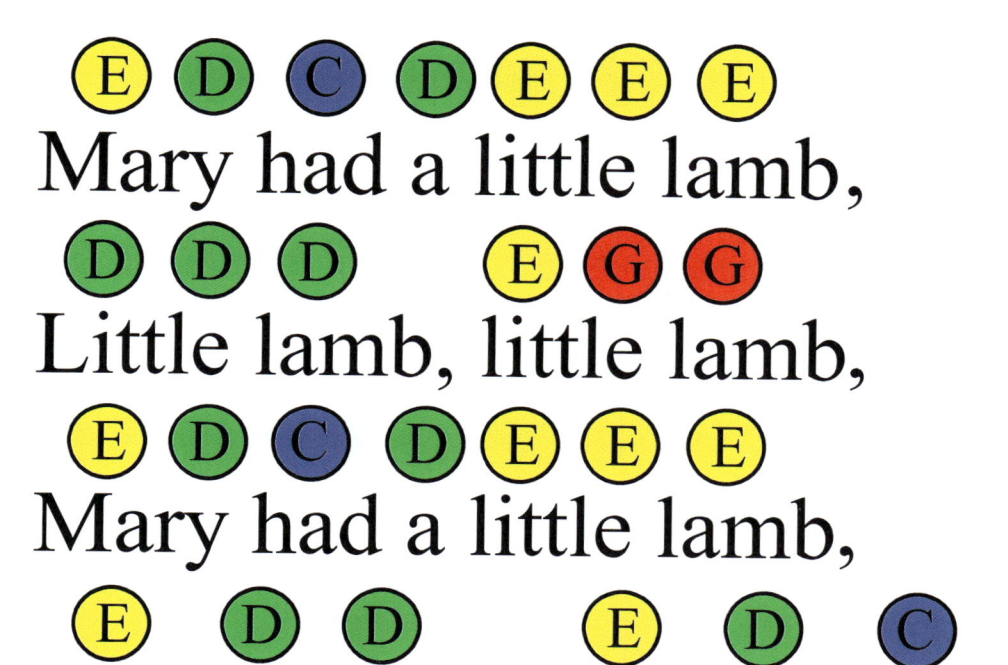

Mary Had a Little Lamb

E D C D E E E
Mary had a little lamb,
D D D   E G G
Little lamb, little lamb,
E D C D E E E
Mary had a little lamb,
E D D   E D C
Its fleece was white as snow.

Mary had a little lamb,
Little lamb, little lamb,
Mary had a little lamb,
Its fleece was white as snow.

The Wheels on the Bus

(C) (F) (F) (F) (F) (A) (C₈) (A) (F)
The wheels on the bus go round and round.

(G) (E) (C) (C₈) (A) (F)
Round and round. Round and round.

(C) (F) (F) (F) (F) (A) (C₈) (A) (F)
The wheels on the bus go round and round.

(G) (C) (C) (F)
All through the town.

The wheels on the bus go round and round.
Round and round.Round and round.
The wheels on the bus go round and round.
All through the town.

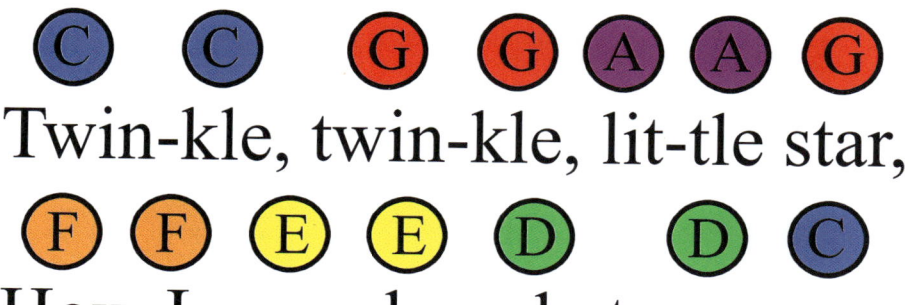

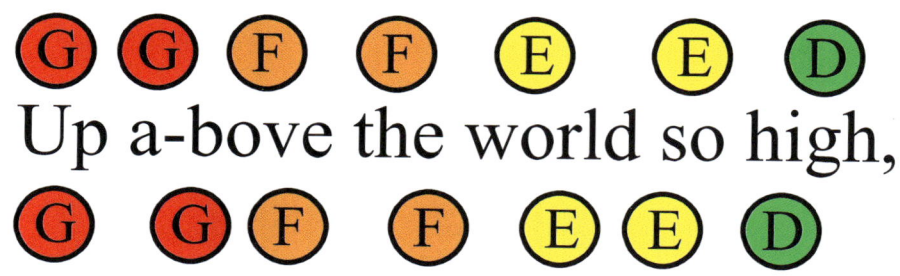

Twinkle, Twinkle, Little Star

C C G G A A G
Twin-kle, twin-kle, lit-tle star,
F F E E D D C
How I won-der what you are.
G G F F E E D
Up a-bove the world so high,
G G F F E E D
Like a dia-mond in the sky.

Twinkle, twinkle, little star,
How I wonder what you are.
Up above the world so high,
Like a diamond in the sky.

Old MacDonald Had a Farm

G G G D E E D
Old McDonald had a farm.

B B A A G
E - I - E - I - O

D G G G D E E D
And on that farm he had a cow.

B B A A G
E - I - E - I - O

D D G G G
With a moo moo here.

D D G G G
With a moo moo here.

What does a cow say?
Meow?
Oink?
Moo?

G G G
Here a moo.

G G G
There a moo.

G G G G G G
Everywhere a moo moo.

G G G D E E D
Old McDonald had a farm.

B B A A G
E - I - E - I - O

6

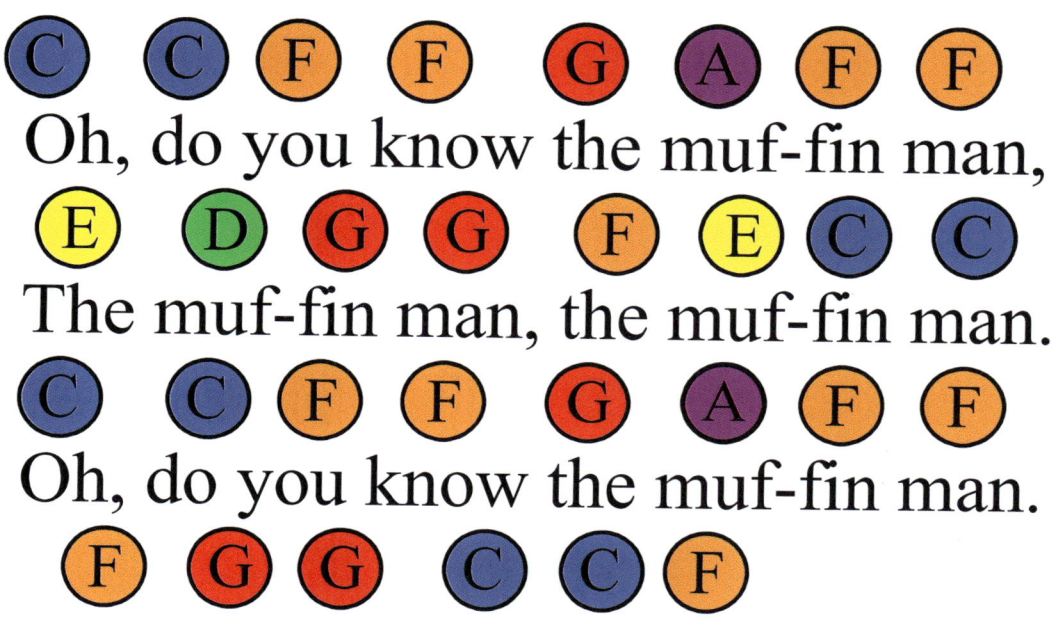

Do You Know the Muffin Man?

(C) (C) (F) (F) (G) (A) (F) (F)
Oh, do you know the muf-fin man,
(E) (D) (G) (G) (F) (E) (C) (C)
The muf-fin man, the muf-fin man.
(C) (C) (F) (F) (G) (A) (F) (F)
Oh, do you know the muf-fin man.
(F) (G) (G) (C) (C) (F)
That lives on Dru-ry Lane?

Oh, do you know the muffin man,
The muffin man, the muffin man.
Oh, do you know the muffin man.
That lives on Drury Lane?

London Bridge is Falling Down

(G) (A) (G) (F) (E) (F) (G)
London Bridge is falling down,
(D) (E) (F) (E) (F) (G)
Falling down, falling down.
(G) (A) (G) (F) (E) (F) (G)
London Bridge is falling down,
(D) (G) (E) (C)
My fair lady.

London Bridge is falling down,
Falling down, falling down.
London Bridge is falling down,
My fair lady.

Jingle Bells

E E E E E E
Jingle bells, jingle bells,

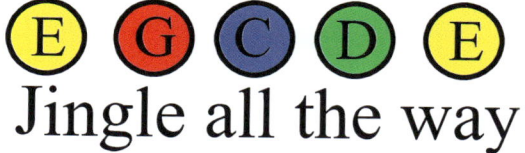

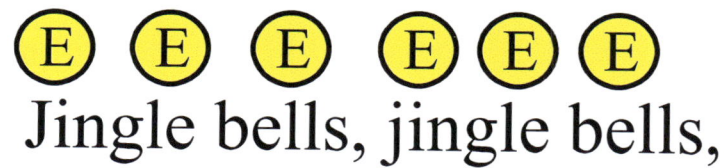

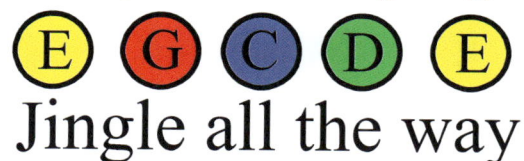

E G C D E
Jingle all the way

F F F F F E E
Oh, what fun it is to ride

E E D D E D G
In a one horse open sleigh.

E E E E E E
Jingle bells, jingle bells,

E G C D E
Jingle all the way

F F F F F E E
Oh, what fun it is to ride

E G G F D C
In a one horse open sleigh.

9

We Wish You a Merry Christmas

C F F G F E D D
We wish you a Mer-ry Christ-mas,

D G G A G F E C
We wish you a Mer-ry Christ-mas,

C A A B A G F D
We wish you a Mer-ry Christ-mas,

C C D G E F
And a Hap-py New Year!

We wish you a Merry Christmas,
We wish you a Merry Christmas,
We wish you a Merry Christmas,
And a Happy New Year!

Brahms' Lullaby
(Lullaby and Goodnight)

E E G E E G
Lullaby, and good night,

E G C₈ B A A G
With pink roses bedight,

D E F D D E F
With lilies o'er spread,

D F B A G B C₈
Is my baby's sweet head.

C C C₈ A F G
Lay you down now, and rest,

E C F G A G
May your slumber be blessed!

C C C₈ A F G
Lay you down now, and rest,

E C F E D C
May your slumber be blessed!

Ode to Joy

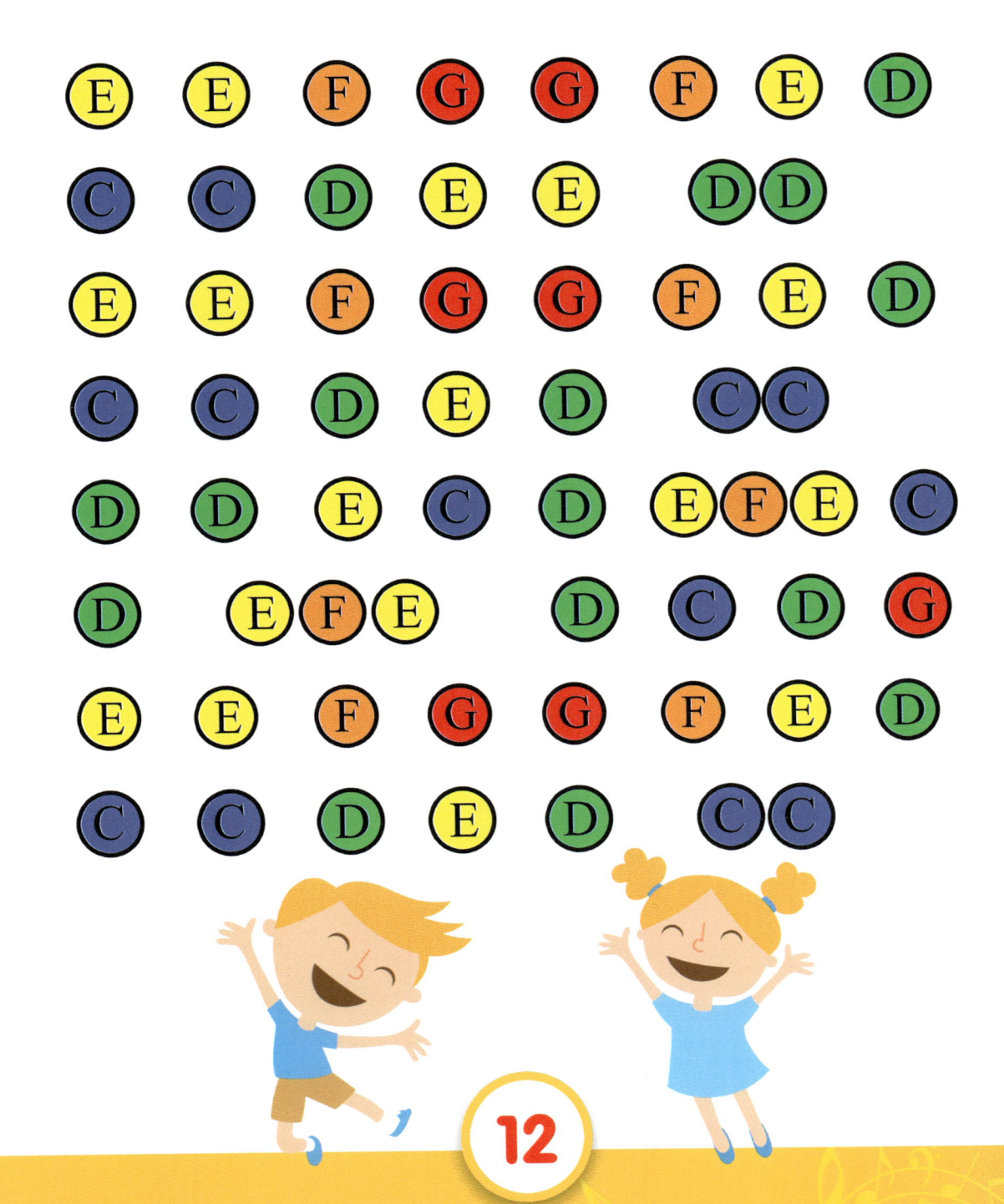

E E F G G F E D
C C D E E D D
E E F G G F E D
C C D E D C C
D D E C D E F E C
D E F E D C D G
E E F G G F E D
C C D E D C C

12

Happy Birthday

C C D C F E
Happy birthday to you,

C C D C G F
Happy birthday to you,

C C C₈ A F F E D
Happy birthday dear Mary,

C₈ C₈ A F G F
Happy birthday to you!

Happy birthday to you,
Happy birthday to you,
Happy birthday dear Mary,
Happy birthday to you!

La Cucaracha

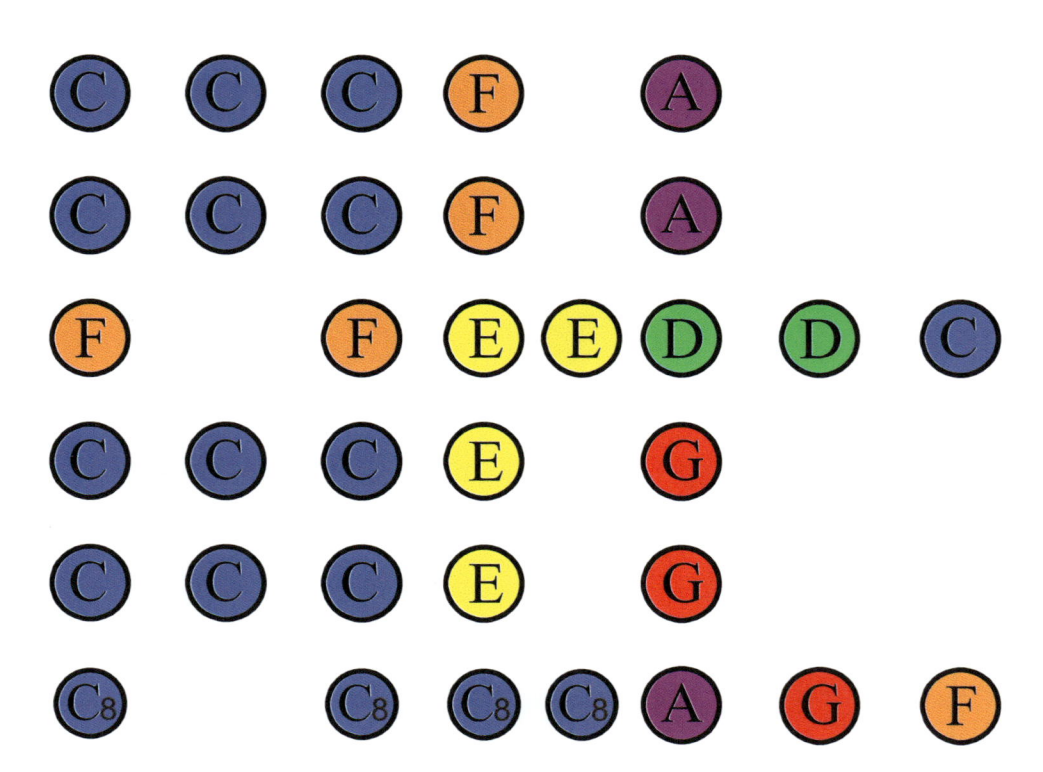

C C C F A
C C C F A
F   F E E D D C
C C C E G
C C C E G
C₈   C₈ C₈ C₈ A G F

14

Oh! Susannah

C D E G G A G E
Oh! I come from A-la-ba-ma
C D E E D C D
With my ban-jo on my knee,
C D E G G A G E
I'm going to Louis-i-a-na
C D E E D D C
My true love for to see.
F F A A
Oh! Su-san-nah,
G G E C D
Don't you cry for me,
C D E G G A G E
I come from A-la-ba-ma
C D E E D D C
With my Ban-jo on my knee.

Oh! I come from Alabama
With my banjo on my knee,
I'm going to Louisiana
My true love for to see.
Oh! Susannah,
Don't you cry for me,
I come from Alabama
With my Banjo on my knee.

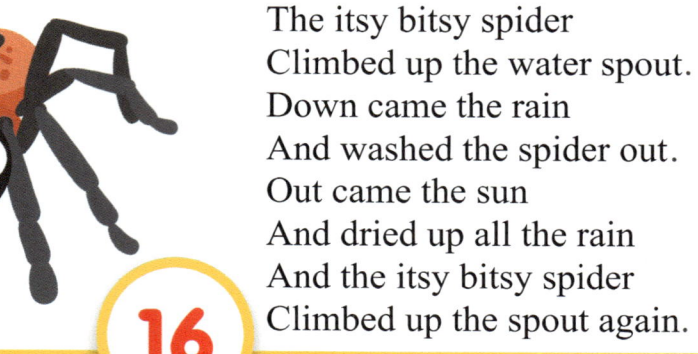

Itsy Bitsy Spider

C C C C D E E
The itsy-bitsy spider
　　E　　D C　D E　C
Climbed up the water spout.
　　E　　E F G
Down came the rain
　　G　F　　E F G E
And washed the spider out.
　　C　　C　D　E
Out came the sun
　　E　D　C D E D
And dried up all the rain
　　C　C　C　C D E E
And the itsy-bitsy spider
　　E　　D C　D　E C
Climbed up the spout again.

The itsy bitsy spider
Climbed up the water spout.
Down came the rain
And washed the spider out.
Out came the sun
And dried up all the rain
And the itsy bitsy spider
Climbed up the spout again.

16

The First Noel

E D C D E F G
The   First No - el,

A B C₈ B A G
The An - gels did say

A B C₈ B A G A B C₈ G F E
Was to cer - tain poor shepherds in fields where they lay,

E D C D E F G
In   fields whe - re they

A B C₈ B A G
Lay keep - ing their sheep

A B C₈ B A G A B C₈ G F E
On a cold win - ter's night that was so deep.

E D C D E F G C₈ B A A G
No - el, No - el, No - el, No - el

C₈ B A G A B C₈ G F E
Born is the King of Is - ra - el!

The First Noel,
The Angels did say
Was to certain poor shepherds in fields as they lay,
In fields where they
Lay keeping their sheep
On a cold winter's night that was so deep.
Noel, Noel, Noel, Noel,
Born is the King of Israel!

Yankee Doodle

C C D E C E D
Yankee Doodle went to town

C C D E C B
Riding on a pony,

C C D E F E D
Stuck a feather in his cap

C₈ B G A B C₈ C₈
And called it macaroni.

A B A G A B C₈
Yankee Doodle keep it up,

G A G F E G
Yankee Doodle dandy,

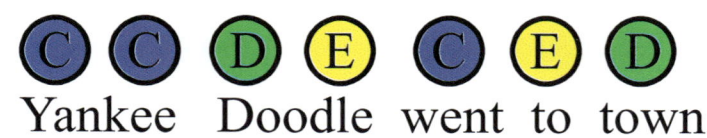

A B A G A B C₈
Mind the music and the step,

A G C₈ B C₈ C₈ C₈
And with the girls be handy.

Yankee Doodle went to town
Riding on a pony,
Stuck a feather in his cap
And called it macaroni.

Yankee Doodle keep it up,
Yankee Doodle dandy,
Mind the music and the step,
And with the girls be handy.

18

Row, Row, Row Your Boat

(C) (C) (C) (D) (E)
Row, row, row your boat,

(E) (D) (E) (F) (G)
Gently down the stream.

(C8)(C8)(C8) (G)(G)(G) (E)(E)(E) (C)(C)(C)
Merrily, merrily, merrily, merrily,

(G) (F) (E) (D) (C)
Life is but a dream.

Row, row, row your boat,
Gently down the stream.
Merrily, merrily, merrily, merrily,
Life is but a dream.

Jolly Old Saint Nicholas

(A) (A) (A) (A)   (G) (G) (G)
Jolly old Saint Nicholas,
(F) (F) (F) (F) (A)
Lean your ear this way.
(D) (D) (D) (D) (C) (C) (F)
Don't you tell a single soul
(G) (F) (G) (A) (G)
What I'm going to say.
(A) (A) (A) (A) (G) (G) (G)
Christmas Eve is coming soon.
(F) (F) (F) (F) (A)
Now, you dear old man,
(D) (D) (D) (D) (C) (C) (F)
Whisper what you'll bring to me.
(G) (F) (G) (A) (F)
Tell me if you can.

Jolly old St. Nicholas,
Lean your ear this way.
Don't you tell a single soul
What I'm going to say.
Christmas Eve is coming soon.
Now, you dear old man,
Whisper what you'll bring to me.
Tell me if you can.

Amazing Grace

C F A A G F D C
Amazing grace! How sweet the sound,

C F A A G C8
That saved a wretch like me.

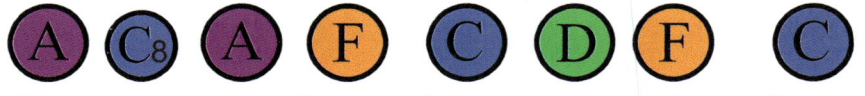

A C8 A F C D F C
I once was lost, but now a'm found,

C F A A G C8
Was blind but now I see.

Amazing grace! How sweet the sound,
That saved a wretch like me.
I once was lost, but now a'm found,
Was blind but now I see.

Copyright by Intemenos.com

All Rights Reserved. No part of this book may be reproduced or utilized in any form or by any means, electronic or mechanical, without permission in writing from the publisher.
Intemenos Ltd. 160 City Road, London, UK

Printed in Great Britain
by Amazon